The Early Church Today Series

St. John Chrysostom

NO ONE CAN HARM THE MAN WHO DOES NOT INJURE HIMSELF

THE EARLY CHURCH TODAY SERIES

Volume 8

The early leaders of the Church, tasked with shepherding Christ's flock, left us spiritual wealth that is too often neglected in modern times. The Early Church Today Series, published by the St. Mary & St. Moses Abbey Press, aims to help make that richness more accessible to readers, inviting them to see the applicability of the early Church to our walk with God today. By sharing practical selections from the writings of the early Church, aided by meaningful editorial supplements and revisions, each book will attempt to diminish impediments and bring to light what the Church has to offer.

ST. MARY & MOSES ABBEY PRESS

No One can Harm the Man
who does not Injure Himself

ST. JOHN CHRYSOSTOM

Translated by
W.R.W. Stephens

Revised by
St. Mary and St. Moses Abbey

No One can Harm the Man who does not Injure Himself

By St. John Chrysostom

Translated by W.R.W. Stephens

Revised by St. Mary and St. Moses Abbey

Minor editing of the original translation was done by St. Mary and St. Moses Abbey, primarily changing archaic words to their modern counterparts. The text was retrieved from: Saint Chrysostom, *Treatise to Prove that no one can Harm the Man who does not Injure Himself.* In *Nicene and Post-Nicene Fathers: First Series* 9, Schaff P., ed. (New York, NY: The Christian Literature Company, 1889), 271–284. The introduction is adapted from the *prolegomena* of the aforesaid book.

Designed & Published by:
St. Mary & St. Moses Abbey Press
101 S Vista Dr, Sandia, TX 78383
stmabbeypress.com

Cover icon of St. John Chrysostom was written by Gergis Samir.

CONTENTS

✠

INTRODUCTION

Who is St. John Chrysostom?

One of the greatest orators and commentators in the entire Christian world, St. John was born in AD 347 at Antioch, the home of the mother Church, where the disciples of Jesus were first called "Christians." His father died during John's infancy, leaving John and his older sister to their young, widowed mother of twenty years. His mother, Anthusa, was a rare woman who refused to be married again, rather devoting herself to the education of John and his sister. She gave her son an admirable education, planting in his soul the seeds of piety. Nevertheless, he was not baptized until he reached the age of maturity.

St. John Chrysostom received his literary training chiefly from Libanius, the first classical scholar and rhetorician of his age. Libanius introduced him to the Greek classics and the arts of rhetoric, which served a good purpose for his future work in the Church. After completing his studies, St. John became a rhetorician and began the profitable practice of the law, which opened to him a brilliant political career. But he was not satisfied, for the temptations of the secular profession in a corrupt state of society discouraged him.

Many factors came together to produce a change in St. John's character: the quiet study of the Scriptures, the example of his pious mother, his acquaintance with Bishop Meletius, and the influence of his close friend Basil, who was of the same age and devoted to the ascetic life. And so he entered the class of the catechumens, and after three years he was baptized by Bishop Meletius at the age of twenty-three. His baptism, like St. Augustine's, was the turning point in his life, a complete dedication to Christ. Concerning his baptism, Palladius says, "But you cannot convince me, that after his baptism John ever swore, or made another swear, or slandered, or lied, or cursed, or indulged in frivolities."[1] Bishop Meletius, who foresaw the future greatness of the young lawyer, wished to secure him for the active service of the Church, and so ordained him as a Reader in about AD 370.

St. John's first inclination after baptism was to abandon the world for the monastic life, but his mother's entreaties prevailed on him to delay the gratification of his desire. Although he yielded to his mother's wishes, he turned his home into a monastery.

---

1   *The Dialogue of Palladius Concerning the Life of Chrysostom*, Herbert-Moore, trans. (New York, NY: The Macmillan Company, 1921), 166.

He secluded himself from the world and practiced a rigid ascetism: eating a little and seldom and only the plainest food, sleeping on the ground, and praying frequently. He also kept almost unbroken silence to avoid falling into slander.

It was during this period of his life that the clergy and the people deemed St. John and his friend Basil, who is not St. Basil the Great, worthy of the episcopal office.[2] St. John, however, escaped being ordained by means of a pious fraud. This led to the writing of one of St. John's greatest works, the six books *On the Priesthood*.

After the death of his mother, St. John Chrysostom fled from the tumults of city life to the monastic solitude of the mountains south of Antioch, and there he spent six happy years, in theological study and sacred meditation and prayer. Monasticism was to him a profitable school of spiritual experience and self-government. He embraced this mode of life as "the true philosophy" from the purest motives. There, the monks lived in separate cells, but according to a common rule and under the authority of an abbot. They wore coarse garments of camel's hair or goat's hair under their linen tunics; they rose up early before

---

2   In *On the Priesthood*, St. John says, "We were both of us disturbed by a report suddenly reaching us that we were about to be advanced to the dignity of the episcopate." Chrysostom, *On the Priesthood* 1.6. (NPNF[1] 9), 34–35. The translator of the *On the Priesthood* wrote, "'The episcapate' is the reading of most mss., but four have 'the priesthood.'"

sunrise for communal prayer and to sing hymns of praise. Their only food was bread and water, except in case of sickness. They slept on straw couches, free from care and anxiety. There was no need for bolts and bars; they held all things in common. For them to live was Christ, and to die was gain.

By excessive self-mortification, St. John undermined his health and returned to Antioch. There he was immediately ordained deacon by Meletius in AD 380 or 381, and a few years afterwards a priest by Flavian in AD 386. He now entered upon a large field of usefulness, the real work of his life. The pulpit was his throne, and he adorned it as much as any preacher of ancient and modern times. St. John Chrysostom preached Sunday after Sunday and during the Great Fast, sometimes twice or more often during the week, even five days in succession, on the duties and responsibilities of Christians, and fearlessly attacked the immorality of the city.

After the death of Nectarius (successor to Gregory Nazianzen), towards the end of the year AD 397, St. Jon Chrysostom was chosen archbishop of Constantinople and was consecrated in AD 398. By his eloquent sermons, he soon gained the admiration of the people and Emperor Arcadius. But he also made enemies by his denunciations of the vices and follies of the clergy and aristocracy. He emptied the episcopal palace of its costly plate and furniture and sold them for the benefit of the poor and the hospitals, and he devoted his large income to benevolence. He refused invitations to banquets, gave no dinner parties, and ate the simplest food in his solitary chamber. He made reforms so severe against lax morals and luxury that his unpopularity increased among the clergy and the Empress Eudoxia who harbored a deep-rooted grudge against him. He was banished more than once, and finally was exiled to the village Cucusus on the borders of Cilicia and Armenia, and from that solitude by his correspondence he exerted a wider influence than from the episcopal throne, between AD 404 and 407. Almost all his letters were from those three years of exile, breathing a noble Christian spirit, in a clear, brilliant, and persuasive style. They exhibit his faithful care for all the interests of the Church and look calmly and hopefully to the glories of heaven. For the consolation of Olympias, the deaconess, a widow of noble birth, he wrote a special treatise on the theme that "No one is really injured except by himself." He died in exile in AD 407, in his sixtieth year, the tenth of his episcopate. His last words were his accustomed doxology, the motto of his life, "Glory be to God for all things. Amen."

NO ONE CAN HARM THE MAN
WHO DOES NOT INJURE HIMSELF

1. I know well that to coarse-minded persons, who are greedy in the pursuit of present things, and are nailed to earth, and enslaved to physical pleasure, and have no strong hold upon spiritual ideas, this treatise will be of a strange and paradoxical kind; and they will laugh immoderately, and condemn me for uttering incredible things from the very outset of my theme. Nevertheless, I shall not on this account desist from my promise, but for this very reason shall proceed with great earnestness to the proof of what I have undertaken. For if those who take that view of my subject will please not to make a clamor and disturbance, but wait to the end of my discourse, I am sure that they will take my side, and condemn themselves, finding that they have been deceived hitherto, and will make a recantation and apology, and beg for pardon for the mistaken opinion which they held concerning these matters, and will express great gratitude to me, as patients do to physicians, when they have been relieved from the disorders which lay siege to their body. For do not tell me of the judgment which is prevailing in your mind at the present time, but wait to hear the contention of my arguments and then you will be able to record an impartial verdict without being hindered by ignorance from forming a true judgment. For even judges in secular causes, if they see the first orator pouring forth a mighty torrent of words and overwhelming everything with his speech do not venture to record their decision without having patiently listened to the other speaker who is opposed to him; and even if the remarks of the

first speaker seem to be just to an unlimited extent, they reserve an unprejudiced hearing for the second. In fact the special merit of judges consists in ascertaining with all possible accuracy what each side has to allege and then bringing forward their own judgment.

Now in the place of an orator we have the common assumption of mankind which in the course of ages has taken deep root in the minds of the multitude, and declaims to the following effect throughout the world. "All things," it says "have been turned upside down, the human race is full of much confusion, and many are they who every day are being wronged, insulted, subjected to violence and injury, the weak by the strong, the poor by the rich: and as it is impossible to number the waves of the sea, so is it impossible to reckon the multitude of those who are the victims of intrigue, insult, and suffering; and neither the correction of law, nor the fear of being brought to trial, nor anything else can arrest this pestilence and disorder, but the evil is increasing every day, and the groans, and lamentations, and weeping of the sufferers are universal; and the judges who are appointed to reform such evils, themselves intensify the tempest, and inflame the disorder, and hence many of the more senseless and despicable kind, seized with a new kind of frenzy, accuse the providence of God, when they see the forbearing man often violently seized, racked, and oppressed, and the audacious, impetuous, low and low-born man waxing rich, and invested with authority, and becoming formidable to many, and inflicting

14

countless troubles upon the more moderate, and this perpetrated both in town and country, and desert, on sea and land." This discourse of ours of necessity comes in by way of direct opposition to what has been alleged, maintaining a contention which is new, as I said at the beginning, and contrary to opinion, yet useful and true, and profitable to those who will give heed to it and be persuaded by it; for what I undertake is to prove (only make no commotion) that no one of those who are wronged is wronged by another, but experiences this injury at his own hands.

2. But in order to make my argument plainer, let us first of all enquire what injustice is, and of what kind of things the material of it is wont to be composed; also what human virtue is, and what it is which ruins it; and further what it is which seems to ruin it but really does not. For instance (for I must complete my argument by means of examples) each thing is subject to one evil which ruins it; iron to rust, wool to moth, flocks of sheep to wolves. The virtue of wine is injured when it ferments and turns sour: of honey when it loses its natural sweetness, and is reduced to a bitter juice. Ears of corn are ruined by mildew and drought, and the fruit, and leaves, and branches of vines by the mischievous host of locusts, other trees by the caterpillar, and irrational creatures by diseases of various kinds; and not to lengthen the list by going through all possible examples, our own flesh is subject to fevers, and palsies, and a crowd of other maladies.

As then each one of these things is liable to that which ruins its virtue, let us now consider what it is which injures the human race, and what it is which ruins the virtue of a human being. Most men think that there are diverse things which have this effect; for I must mention the erroneous opinions on the subject, and, after confuting them, proceed to exhibit that which really does ruin our virtue, and to demonstrate clearly that no one could inflict this injury or bring this ruin upon us unless we betrayed ourselves. The multitude then having erroneous opinions imagine that there are many different things which ruin our virtue: some say it is poverty, others bodily disease, others loss of property, others calumny, others death and they are perpetually bewailing and lamenting these things; and whilst they are commiserating the sufferers and shedding tears they excitedly exclaim to one another, "What a calamity has befallen such and such a man! He has been deprived of all his fortune at a blow." Of another again one will say, "Such and such a man has been attacked by severe sickness and is despaired of by the physicians in attendance." Some bewail and lament the inmates of the prison, some those who have been expelled from their country and transported to the land of exile, others those who have been deprived of their freedom, others those who have been seized and made captives by enemies, others those who have been drowned, or burnt, or buried by the fall of a house, but no one mourns those who are living in wickedness; on the contrary, which is worse than all, they often congratulate them, a practice which is the cause of all manner of evils. Come then (only, as I exhorted you at the outset, do not make a commotion), let me prove that none of the things which have been mentioned injure the man who lives soberly, nor can ruin his virtue. For tell me if a man has lost his all, either at the hands of calumniators or of robbers, or has been stripped of his goods by knavish servants, what harm has the loss done to the virtue of the man?

But if it seems well, let me rather indicate in the first place what is the virtue of a man, beginning by dealing with the subject in the case of existences of another kind so as to make it more intelligible and plain to the majority of readers.

3. What then is the virtue of a horse? Is it to have a bridle studded with gold and girths to match, and a band of silken threads to fasten the housing, and clothes wrought in divers colors and gold tissue, and headgear studded with jewels, and locks of hair plaited with gold cord? Or is it to be swift and strong in its legs, and even in its paces, and to have hoofs suitable to a well-bred horse, and courage fitted for long journeys and warfare, and to be able to behave with calmness in the battlefield, and if a rout takes place to save its rider? Is it not manifest that these are the things which constitute the virtue of the horse, not the others?

Again, what should you say was the virtue of donkeys and mules? Is it not the power of carrying burdens with contentment, and accomplishing journeys with ease, and having hoofs like rock? Shall we say that their outside trappings contribute anything to their own proper virtue? By no means. And what kind of vine shall we admire? One which abounds in leaves and branches, or one which is laden with fruit? Or what kind of virtue do we predicate of an olive? Is it to have large boughs, and great luxuriance of leaves, or to exhibit an abundance of its proper fruit dispersed over all parts of the tree?

Well, let us act in the same way in the case of human beings also: let us determine what is the virtue of man, and let us regard that alone as an injury, which is destructive to it. What then is the virtue of man? Not riches that you should fear poverty, nor health of body that you should dread sickness; nor the opinion of the public, that you should view an evil reputation with alarm; nor life simply for its own sake, that death should be terrible to you; nor liberty that you should avoid servitude; but carefulness in holding true doctrine, and rectitude in life. Of these things, not even the devil himself will be able to rob a man, if he who possesses them guards them with the needful carefulness, and that most malicious and ferocious demon is aware of this.

For this cause also he robbed Job of his substance, not to make him poor, but that he might force him into uttering some blasphemous speech; and he tortured his body, not to subject him to infirmity, but to upset the virtue of his soul. But nevertheless when he had set all his devices in motion, and turned him from a rich man into a poor one (that calamity which seems to us the most terrible of all), and had made him childless who was once surrounded by many children, and had scarified his whole body more cruelly than the executioners do in the public tribunals (for their nails do not lacerate the sides of those who fall into their hands so severely as the gnawing of the worms lacerated his body), and when he had fastened a bad reputation upon him (for Job's friends who were present with him said, "You have not received the chastisement which your sins deserve," and directed many words of accusation against him), and after he had not merely expelled him from city and home and transferred him to another city, but had actually made the dunghill serve as his home and city; after all this, he not only did him no damage but rendered him more glorious by the designs which he formed against him. And he not only failed to rob him of any of his possessions, although he had robbed him of so many things, but he even increased the wealth of his virtue. For after these things he enjoyed greater confidence inasmuch as he had contended in a more severe contest.

Now if he who underwent such sufferings, and this not at the hand of man, but at the hand of the devil who is more wicked than all men, sustained no injury, which of those persons who say, "Such and such a man injured and damaged me," will have any defense to make in the future? For if the devil who is full of such great malice, after having set all his instruments in motion, and discharged all his weapons, and poured out all the evils incident to man, in a superlative degree upon the family and the person of that righteous man nevertheless did him no injury, but as I was saying rather profited him: how shall certain be able to accuse such and such a man alleging that they have suffered injury at their hands, not at their own?

4. What then? Someone will say, "Did he not inflict injury on Adam, and upset him, and cast him out of paradise?" No, he did not do it, but the cause was the listlessness of him who was injured, and his want of temperance and vigilance. For he who applied such powerful and manifold devices and yet was not able to subdue Job, how could he by inferior means have mastered Adam, had not Adam betrayed himself through his own listlessness? What then? Has he not been injured who has been exposed to slander, and suffered confiscation of his property, having been deprived of all his goods, and is thrown out of his patrimony, and struggles with extreme poverty? No! He has not been injured, but has even profited, if he be sober. For, tell me, what harm did this do the apostles? Were they not continually struggling with hunger, and thirst, and nakedness? And this was the very reason why they were so illustrious, and distinguished, and won for themselves much help from God.

Again what harm was done to Lazarus by his disease, and sores, and poverty, and lack of protectors? Were they not the reasons why garlands of victory were more abundantly woven for him? Or what harm was done to Joseph by his getting evil reported of, both in his own land, and in the land of strangers, for he was supposed to be both an adulterer and fornicator? Or what harm did servitude do him or expatriation? Is it not especially on account of these things that we regard him with admiration and astonishment? And why do I speak of removal into a foreign land, and poverty, and evil report, and bondage? For what harm did death itself inflict on Abel, although it was a violent and untimely death, and perpetrated by a brother's hand? Is this not the reason why his praise is sounded throughout the whole world?

See how the discourse has demonstrated even more than it promised? For not only has it disclosed the fact that no one is injured by anybody, but also that they who take heed to themselves derive the greater gain (from such assaults). What is the purpose then it will be said of penalties and punishments? What is the purpose of hell? What is the purpose of such great threatenings, if no one is either injured or injures? What is it you say? Why do you confuse the argument? For I did not say that no one injures, but that no one is injured. And how is it possible, you will say, for no one to be injured when many are committing injury? In the way that I indicated just now. For Joseph's brethren did indeed injure him, yet he himself was not injured; and Cain laid snares for Abel, yet he himself was not ensnared. This is the reason why there are penalties and punishments. For God does not abolish penalties on account of the virtue of those who suffer; but he ordains punishments on account of the malice of those who do wickedly. For although they who are evil-treated become more illustrious in consequence of the designs formed against them, this is not due to the intention of those who plan the designs, but to the courage of those who are the victims of them. Wherefore for the latter the rewards of philosophy are made ready and prepared, for the former the penalties of wickedness.

Have you been deprived of your money? Read the word, "Naked came I out of my mother's womb, and naked shall I return there."[3] And add to this the apostolic saying, "For we brought nothing into this world; it is certain we can carry nothing out."[4] Are you evil reported of, and have some men loaded you with countless abuse? Remember that passage where it is said, "Woe unto you when all men shall speak well of you,"[5] and "Rejoice and leap for joy when they shall cast upon you an evil name."[6] Have you been transported into the land of exile? Consider that you have not here a fatherland, but that if you will be wise, you are bidden to regard the whole world as a strange country. Or have you been given over to a sore disease? Quote the apostolic saying, "The more our outward man decays, so much the more is the inward man renewed day by day."[7] Has anyone suffered a violent death? Consider the case of John, his head cut off in prison, carried in

---

3   Job 1:21.
4   1 Timothy 6:7.
5   Luke 6:26.
6   Cf. Matthew 5:11 and Luke 6:22.
7   2 Corinthians 4:16.

a platter, and made the reward of a harlot's dancing. Consider the recompense which is derived from these things: for all these sufferings when they are unjustly inflicted by anyone on another, expiate sins, and work righteousness. So great is the advantage of them in the case of those who bear them bravely.

5. When then neither loss of money, nor slander, nor railing, nor banishment, nor diseases, nor tortures, nor that which seems more formidable than all, namely death, harms those who suffer them, but rather adds to their profit, whence can you prove to me that any one is injured when he is not injured at all from any of these things? For I will endeavor to prove the reverse, showing that they who are most injured and insulted, and suffer the most incurable evils, are the persons who do these things. For what could be more miserable than the condition of Cain, who dealt with his brother in this fashion? What more pitiable than that of Phillip's wife who beheaded John? Or the brethren of Joseph who sold him away, and transported him into the land of exile? Or the devil who tortured Job with such great calamities? For not only on account of his other iniquities, but at the same time also for this assault, he will pay no trifling penalty. Do you see how here the argument has proved even more than was proposed, showing that those who are insulted not only sustain no harm from these assaults, but that the whole mischief recoils on the head of those who contrive them?

For since neither wealth nor freedom, nor life in our native land, nor the other things which I have mentioned, but only right actions of the soul, constitute the virtue of man, naturally when the harm is directed against these things, human virtue itself is no wise harmed. What then? Supposing someone does harm the moral condition of the soul? Even then if a man suffers damage, the damage does not come from another but proceeds from within, and from the man himself. "How so," do you say? When anyone having been beaten by another, or deprived of his goods, or having endured some other grievous insult, utters a blasphemous speech, he certainly sustains a damage thereby, and a very great one, nevertheless it does not proceed from him who has inflicted the insult, but from his own littleness of soul. For what I said before I will now repeat, no man if he be infinitely wicked could attack any one more wickedly or more bitterly than that revengeful demon who is implacably hostile to us, the devil, but yet this cruel demon had not power to upset or overthrow him who lived before the law, and before the time of grace, although he discharged so many and such bitter weapons against him from all quarters. Such is the force of nobility of soul.

And what shall I say of Paul? Did he not suffer so many distresses that even to make a list of them is no easy matter? He was put in prison, loaded with chains, dragged here and there, scourged by the Jews, stoned, lacerated on the back not only by whips, but also by rods, he was immersed in the sea, oftentimes beset by robbers, involved in strife with his own countrymen, continually assailed both by foes and by acquaintance, subjected to countless intrigues, struggling with hunger and nakedness, undergoing other frequent and lasting mischances and afflictions: and why need I mention the greater part of them? He was dying every day, but yet, although subjected to so many and such grievous sufferings, he not only uttered no blasphemous word, but rejoiced over these things and gloried in them; and one time he says, "I rejoice in my sufferings,"[8] and then again, "Not only this but we also glory in afflictions."[9] If then he rejoiced and gloried when suffering such great troubles, what excuse will you have, and what defense will you make if you blaspheme when you do not undergo the smallest fraction of them.

6. But I am injured in other ways, one will say, and even if I do not blaspheme, yet when I am robbed of my money, I am disabled from giving alms. This is a mere pretext and pretense. For if you grieve on this account, know certainly that poverty is no bar to almsgiving. For even if you are infinitely poor you are not poorer than the woman who possessed only a handful of meal,[10] and the one who had only two mites,[11] each of whom having spent all her substance upon those who were in need was an object of surpassing admiration; and such great poverty was no hindrance to such great

---

8   Colossians 1:24.

9   Romans 5:3.

10   See 1 Kings 17:12.

11   See Luke 21:2.

lovingkindness, but the alms bestowed from the two mites was so abundant and generous as to eclipse all who had riches, and in wealth of intention and superabundance of zeal to surpass those who cast in much coin. Wherefore even in this matter, you are not injured but rather benefitted, receiving by means of a small contribution rewards more glorious than they who put down large sums.

But since, if I were to say these things forever, sensuous characters which delight to grovel in worldly things, and revel in present things would not readily endure parting from the fading flowers (for such are the pleasant things of this life) or letting go its shadows, but the better sort of men indeed cling to both the one and the other, while the more pitiable and abject cling more strongly to the former than to the latter, come let us strip off the pleasant and showy masks which hide the base and ugly countenance of these things, and let us expose the foul deformity of the harlot. For such is the character of a life of this kind which is devoted to luxury, and wealth, and power: it is foul and ugly and full of much abomination, disagreeable and burdensome, and charged with bitterness. For this indeed is the special feature in this life which deprives those who are captivated by it of every excuse, that although it is the aim of their longings and endeavors, yet is it filled with much annoyance and bitterness, and teems with innumerable evils, dangers, bloodshed, precipices, crags, murders, fears and tremblings, envy and ill-will, and intrigue, perpetual anxiety and care, and derives no profit, and produces no fruit from these great evils save punishment and revenge, and incessant torment. But although this is its character, it seems to be to most men an object of ambition, and eager contention, which is a sign of the folly of those who are captivated by it, not of the blessedness of the thing itself. Little children indeed are eager and excited about toys and cannot take notice of the things which become full-grown men. There is an excuse for them on account of their immaturity, but these others are debarred from the right of defense, because, although of full age, they are childish in disposition, and more foolish than children in their manner of life.

Now tell me why wealth is an object of ambition? For it is necessary to start from this point, because to the majority of those who are afflicted with this grievous malady it seems to be more precious than health and life, and public reputation, and good opinion, and country, and household, and friends, and kindred, and everything else. Moreover, the flame has ascended to the very clouds, and this fierce heat has taken possession of land and sea. Nor is there anyone to quench this fire, but all people are engaged in stirring it up, both those who have already been caught by it, and those who have not yet been caught, in order that they may be captured. And you may see everyone, husband and wife, household slave, and freeman, rich and poor, each according to his ability carrying loads which supply much fuel to this fire by day and night: loads not of wood or bundles of sticks (for the fire is not of that kind), but loads

27

of souls and bodies, of unrighteousness and iniquity. For such is the material of which a fire of this kind is wont to be kindled. For those who have riches place no limit anywhere to this monstrous passion, even if they compass the whole world; and the poor press on to get in advance of them, and a kind of incurable craze, and unrestrainable frenzy and irremediable disease possesses the souls of all. And this affection has conquered every other kind and thrust it away, expelling it from the soul: neither friends nor kindred are taken into account: and why do I speak of friends and kindred? Not even wife and children are regarded, and what can be dearer to man than these? But all things are dashed to the ground and trampled underfoot, when this savage and inhuman mistress has laid hold of the souls of all who are taken captive by her. For as an inhuman mistress, and harsh tyrant, and savage barbarian, and public and expensive prostitute she debases and exhausts and punishes with innumerable dangers and torments those who have chosen to be in bondage to her; and yet although she is terrible and harsh, and fierce and cruel, and has the face of a barbarian, or rather of a wild beast, fiercer than a wolf or a lion, she seems to those who have been taken captive by her gentle and loveable, and sweeter than honey. And although she forges swords and weapons against them every day, and digs pitfalls and leads them to precipices and crags, and weaves endless snares of punishment for them, yet is she supposed to make these things objects of ambition to those who have been made captive, and those who are desiring to be captured.

And just as a sow delights and revels in wallowing in the ditch and mire, and beetles delight in perpetually crawling over dung, even so they who are captivated by the love of money are more miserable than these creatures. For the abomination is greater in this case, and the mire more offensive; for they who are addicted to this passion imagine that much pleasure is derived from it, which does not arise from the nature of the thing, but of the understanding which is afflicted with such an irrational taste. And this taste is worse in their case than in that of brutes; for as with the mire and the dung, the cause of pleasure is not in them, but in the irrational nature of the creatures who plunge into it; even so count it to be in the case of human beings.

7. And how might we cure those who are thus disposed? It would be possible if they would open their ears to us, and unfold their heart, and receive our words. For it is impossible to turn and divert the irrational animals from their unclean habit; for they are destitute of reason, but this the gentlest of all tribes, honored by reason and speech, I mean human nature, might, if it chose, readily and easily be released from the mire and the stench, and the dung hill and its abomination. For wherefore, O man, do riches seem to you worthy such diligent pursuit? Is it on account of the pleasure which no doubt is derived from the table? Or on account of the honor and the escort of those who pay court to you, because of your wealth? Is it because you are able to defend yourself against those who annoy you, and to be an object of fear

to all? For you cannot name any other reasons, save pleasure and flattery, and fear, and the power of taking revenge; for wealth is not generally wont to make any one wiser, or more self-controlled, or more gentle, or more intelligent, or kind, or benevolent, or superior to anger, or gluttony or pleasure; it does not train any one to be moderate, or teach him how to be humble, nor introduce and implant any other piece of virtue in the soul. Neither could you say for which of these things it deserves to be so diligently sought and desired. For not only is it ignorant how to plant and cultivate any good thing, but even if it finds a store of them, it mars and stunts and blights them; and some of them it even uproots, and introduces their opposites, unmeasured licentiousness, unseasonable wrath, unrighteous anger, pride, arrogance, foolishness. But let me not speak of these; for they who have been seized by this malady will not endure to hear about virtue and vice, being entirely abandoned to pleasure and therefore enslaved to it.

Come then let us forego for the time being the consideration of these points, and let us bring forward the others which remain, and see whether wealth has any pleasure, or any honor; for in my eyes the case is quite the reverse. And first of all, if you please, let us investigate the meals of rich and poor, and ask the guests which they are who enjoy the purest and most genuine pleasure; is it they who recline for a full day on couches, and join breakfast and dinner together, and distend their stomach, and blunt their senses, and sink the vessel by an overladen cargo of food, and waterlog the ship, and drench it as in some shipwreck of the body, and devise fetters, and manacles, and gags, and bind their whole body with the band of drunkenness and surfeit more grievous than an iron chain, and enjoy no sound pure sleep undisturbed by frightful dreams, and are more miserable than madmen and introduce a kind of self-imposed demon into the soul and display themselves as a laughing stock to the gaze of their servants, or rather to the kinder sort amongst them as a tragical spectacle eliciting tears, and cannot recognize any of those who are present, and are incapable of speaking or hearing but have to be carried away from their couches to their bed;—or is it they who are sober and vigilant, and limit their eating by their need, and sail with a favorable breeze, and find hunger and thirst the best relish in their food and drink? For nothing is so conducive to enjoyment and health as to be hungry and thirsty when one attacks the food items, and to identify satiety with the simple necessity of food, never overstepping the limits of this, nor imposing a load upon the body too great for its strength.

8. But if you disbelieve my statement, study the physical condition, and the soul of each class. Are not the bodies vigorous of those who live thus moderately (for do not tell me of that which rarely happens, although some may be weak from some other circumstance, but form your judgment from those instances which are of constant occurrence), I say are they not vigorous, and their senses clear, fulfilling their proper function with much ease?

whereas the bodies of the others are flaccid and softer than wax, and beset with a crowd of maladies? For gout soon fastens upon them, and untimely palsy, and premature old age, and headache, and flatulence, and feebleness of digestion, and loss of appetite, and they require constant attendance of physicians, and perpetual dosing, and daily care. Are these things pleasurable? tell me. Who of those that know what pleasure really is would say so? For pleasure is produced when desire leads the way, and fruition follows: now if there is fruition, but desire is nowhere to be found, the conditions of pleasure fail and vanish. On this account also invalids, although the most charming food is set before them, partake of it with a feeling of disgust and sense of oppression, because there is no desire which gives a keen relish to the enjoyment of it. For it is not the nature of the food, or of the drink, but the appetite of the eaters which is wont to produce the desire, and is capable of causing pleasure. Therefore also a certain wise man, who had an accurate knowledge of all that concerned pleasure, and understood how to moralize about these things, said, "The full soul mocks at honeycombs,"[12] showing that the conditions of pleasure consist not in the nature of the meal, but in the disposition of the eaters. Therefore also the prophet recounting the wonders in Egypt and in the desert mentioned this in connection with the others: "He satisfied them

---

12   Proverbs 27:7 LXX.

with honey out of the rock."[13] And yet nowhere does it appear that honey actually sprang forth for them out of the rock; what then is the meaning of the expression? Because the people being exhausted by much toil and long travelling, and distressed by great thirst rushed to the cool spring, their craving for drink serving as a relish, the writer wishing to describe the pleasures which they received from those fountains called the water honey, not meaning that the element was converted into honey, but that the pleasure received from the water rivalled the sweetness of honey, inasmuch as those who partook of it rushed to it in their eagerness to drink.

Since then these things are so and no one can deny it, however stupid he may be: is it not perfectly plain that pure, undiluted, and lively pleasure is to be found at the tables of the poor? whereas at the tables of the rich there is discomfort, and disgust, and defilement? as that wise man has said, "Even sweet things seem to be a vexation."[14]

9. But riches someone will say procure honor for those who possess them, and enable them to take vengeance on their enemies with ease. And is this a reason, pray, why riches seem to you desirable and worth contending for;—that they nourish the most dangerous passion in our nature, leading on anger into action, swelling the empty bubbles of ambition, and

---

13   Psalms 81:16.

14   See Proverbs 27:7 LXX.

stimulating and urging men to arrogance? Why these are just the very reasons why we ought resolutely to turn our backs upon riches, because they introduce certain fierce and dangerous wild beasts into our heart depriving us of the real honor which we might receive from all, and introducing to deluded men another which is the opposite of this, only painted over with its colors, and persuading them to fancy that it is the same, when by nature it is not so, but only seems to be so to the eye. For as the beauty of courtesans, made up as it is of dyes and pigments, is destitute of real beauty, yet makes a foul and ugly face appear fair and beautiful to those who are deluded by it when it is not so in reality, even so also riches force flattery to look like honor. For I beg you not to consider the praises which are openly bestowed through fear and fawning: for these are only tints and pigments; but unfold the conscience of each of those who flatter you in this fashion, and inside it you will see countless accusers declaring against you, and loathing and detesting you more than your bitterest adversaries and foes. And if ever a change of circumstances should occur which would remove and expose this mask which fear has manufactured, just as the sun when it emits a hotter ray than usual discloses the real countenances of those women whom I mentioned, then you will see clearly that all through the former time you were held in the greatest contempt by those who paid court to you, and you fancied you were enjoying honor from those who thoroughly hated you, and in their heart poured infinite abuse upon you, and longed to see you involved in extreme calamities. For there is nothing like virtue to produce honor,— honor neither forced nor feigned, nor hidden under a mask of deceit, but real and genuine, and able to stand the test of hard times.

10. But do you wish to take vengeance on those who have annoyed you? This, as I was saying just now, is the very reason why wealth ought specially to be avoided. For it prepares you to thrust the sword against yourself, and renders you liable to a heavier account in the future day of reckoning, and makes your punishment intolerable. For revenge is so great an evil that it actually revokes the mercy of God, and cancels the forgiveness of countless sins which has been already bestowed. For he who received remission of the debt of ten thousand talents, and after having obtained so great a favor by merely asking for it then made a demand of one hundred pence from his fellow servant, a demand, that is, for satisfaction for his transgression against himself, in his severity towards his fellow servant recorded his own condemnation; and for this reason and no other he was delivered to the tormentors, and racked, and required to pay back the ten thousand talents; and he was not allowed the benefit of any excuse or defense, but suffered the most extreme penalty, having been commanded to deposit the whole debt which the lovingkindness of God had formerly remitted.[15] Is this then the reason, pray, why wealth is so earnestly pursued by you, because it so

---

15   See Matthew 18:23–35.

easily conducts you into sin of this kind? No truly, this is why you ought to abhor it as a foe and an adversary teeming with countless murders.

But poverty, someone will say, disposes men to be discontented and often also to utter profane words, and condescend to mean actions. It is not poverty which does this, but littleness of soul: for Lazarus also was poor, yes! very poor: and besides poverty, he suffered from infirmity, a bitterer trial than any form of poverty, and one which makes poverty more severely felt; and in addition to infirmity, there was a total absence of protectors, and difficulty in finding any to supply his needs, which increased the bitterness of poverty and infirmity. For each of these things is painful in itself, but when there are none to minister to the sufferer's wants, the suffering becomes greater, the flame more painful, the distress more bitter, the tempest fiercer, the billows stronger, the furnace hotter. And if one examines the case thoroughly, there was yet a fourth trial besides these—the unconcern and luxury of the rich man who dwelt close by. And if you would find a fifth thing, serving as fuel to the flame, you will see quite clearly that he was beset by it. For not only was that rich man living luxuriously, but twice, and thrice, or rather indeed several times in the day he saw the poor man: for he had been laid at his gate, being a grievous spectacle of pitiable distress, and the bare sight of him was sufficient to soften even a heart of stone, and yet even this did not induce that unmerciful man to assist this case of poverty; but he had his luxurious table spread, and goblets wreathed with flowers, and pure wine plentifully poured forth, and grand armies of cooks, and parasites, and flatterers from early dawn, and troops of singers, cupbearers, and jesters; and he spent all his time in devising every species of dissipation, and drunkenness, and surfeiting, and in reveling in dress and feasting and many other things. But although he saw that poor man every day distressed by grievous hunger and the bitterest infirmity, and the oppression of his many sores, and by destitution, and the ills which result from these things, he never even gave him a thought: yet the parasites and the flatterers were pampered even beyond their need; but the poor man, and he so very poor, and encompassed with so many miseries, was not even vouchsafed the crumbs which fell from that table, although he greatly desired them: and yet none of these things injured him, he did not give vent to a bitter word, he did not utter a profane speech; but like a piece of gold which shines all the more brilliantly when it is purified by excessive heat, even so he, although oppressed by these sufferings, was superior to all of them, and to the agitation which in many cases is produced by them. For if generally speaking poor men, when they see rich men, are consumed with envy and racked by malicious ill-will, and deem life not worth living, and this even when they are well supplied with necessary food, and have persons to minister to their needs; what would the condition of this poor man have been had he not been very wise and noble hearted, seeing that he was poor beyond all other poor men, and not only poor, but also infirm, and without any one to protect or cheer him, and lay in the midst of the city as if in a remote desert, and wasted away with bitter hunger, and saw all good things being poured upon the rich man as out of a fountain, and had not the benefit of any human consolation, but lay exposed as a perpetual meal for the tongues of the dogs, for he was so enfeebled and broken down in body that he could not scare them away? Do you perceive that he who does not injure himself suffers no evil? For I will again take up the same argument.

11. For what harm was done to this hero by his bodily infirmity? or by the absence of protectors? or by the coming of the dogs? or the evil proximity of the rich man? or by the great luxury, haughtiness, and arrogance of the latter? Did it weaken him for the contest on behalf of virtue? Did it ruin his fortitude? Nowhere was he harmed at all, but that multitude of sufferings, and the cruelty of the rich man, rather increased his strength and became the pledge for him of infinite crowns of victory, a means of adding to his rewards, an augmentation of his recompense, and a promise of an increased requital. For he was crowned not merely on account of his poverty, or of his hunger or of his sores, or of the dogs licking them: but because, having such a neighbor as the rich man, and being seen by him every day, and perpetually overlooked he endured this trial bravely and with much fortitude, a trial which added no small flame but in fact a very strong one to the fire of poverty, and infirmity and loneliness.

And, tell me, what was the case of the blessed Paul? For there is nothing to prevent my making mention of him again. Did he not experience innumerable storms of trial? And in what respect was he injured by them? Was he not crowned with victory all the more in consequence,—because he suffered hunger, because he was consumed with cold and nakedness, because he was often tortured with the scourge, because he was stoned, because he was cast into the sea? But then someone says that he was Paul, and called by Christ. Yet Judas also was one of the twelve, and he too was called of Christ; but neither his being of the twelve nor his call profited him, because he had not a mind disposed to virtue. But Paul although struggling with hunger, and at a loss to procure necessary food, and daily undergoing such great sufferings, pursued with great zeal the road which leads to heaven, whereas Judas although he had been called before him, and enjoyed the same advantages as he did, and was initiated in the highest form of Christian life, and partook of the holy table and that most awesome of sacred feasts, and received such grace as to be able to raise the dead, and cleanse the lepers, and cast out devils, and often heard discourses concerning poverty, and spent so long a time in the company of Christ Himself, and was entrusted with the money of the poor, so that his passion might be soothed thereby (for he was a thief) even then did not become any better, although he had been favored with such great condescension. For since Christ knew that he was covetous, and destined to perish on account of his love of money, He not only did not demand punishment of him for this at that time, but with a view to softening down his passion he was entrusted with the money of the poor, that having some means of appeasing his greed he might be saved from falling into that appalling gulf of sin, checking the greater evil beforehand by a lesser one.

12. Thus, in no case will anyone be able to injure a man who does not choose to injure himself, but if a man is not willing to be temperate, and to aid himself from his own resources, no one will ever be able to profit him. Therefore also that wonderful history of the Holy Scriptures, as in some lofty, large, and broad picture, has portrayed the lives of the men of old time, extending the narrative from Adam to the coming of Christ; and it exhibits to you both those who are upset, and those who are crowned with victory in the contest, in order that it may instruct you by means of all examples that no one will be able to injure one who is not injured by himself, even if all the world were to kindle a fierce war against him. For it is not stress of circumstances, nor variation of seasons, nor insults of men in power, nor intrigues besetting you like snow storms, nor a crowd of calamities, nor a promiscuous collection of all the ills to which mankind is subject, which can disturb even slightly the man who is brave, and temperate, and watchful; just as on the contrary the indolent and spineless man who is his own betrayer cannot be made better, even with the aid of innumerable ministrations.

This at least was made manifest to us by the parable of the two men, of whom the one built his house upon the rock, the other upon the sand:[16] not that we are to think of sand and rock, or of a building of stone, and a roof, or of rivers, and rain, and wild winds, beating against the buildings, but we are to extract virtue and vice as the meaning of these things, and to perceive from them that no one injures a man who does not injure himself. Therefore, neither the rain although driven furiously along, nor the streams dashing against it with much vehemence, nor the wild winds beating against it with a mighty rush, shook the one house in any degree, but it remained undisturbed, unmoved, that you might understand that no trial can agitate the man who does not betray himself. But the house of the other man was easily swept away, not on account of the force of the trials (for in that case the other would have experienced the same fate), but on account of his own folly; for it did not fall because the wind blew upon it, but because it was built upon the sand, that is to say upon indolence and iniquity. For before that tempest beat upon it, it was weak and ready to fall. For buildings of that kind, even if no one puts any pressure on them, fall to pieces of themselves, the foundation sinking and giving way in every direction. And just as cobwebs part asunder, although no strain is put upon them, but adamant[17] remains unshaken even when it is struck, even so also they who do not injure themselves

---

16   See Matthew 7:24.

17   A type of rock.

become stronger, even if they receive innumerable blows; but they who betray themselves, even if there is no one to harass them, fall of themselves, and collapse and perish. For even thus did Judas perish, not only having been unassailed by any trial of this kind, but having actually enjoyed the benefit of much assistance.

13. Would you like me to illustrate this argument in the case of whole nations? What great forethought was bestowed upon the Jewish nation! Was not the whole visible creation arranged with a view to their service? Was not a new and strange method of life introduced amongst them? For they did not have to send down to a market, and so they had the benefit of things which are sold for money without paying any price for them; neither did they cleave furrows nor drag a plough, nor harrow the ground, nor cast in seed, nor had they need of rain and wind, and annual seasons, nor sunshine, nor phases of the moon, nor climate, nor anything of that kind; they prepared no threshing floor, they threshed no grain, they used no winnowing fan for separating the grain from the chaff, they turned no mill-stone, they built no oven, they brought neither wood nor fire into the house, they needed no baker's art, they handled no spade, they sharpened no sickle, they required no other art, I mean of weaving or building or supplying shoes: but the word of God was everything to them. And they had a table prepared off hand, free of all toil and labor. For such was the nature of the manna; it was new and fresh, nowhere costing them any trouble, nor straining them by labor. And their

clothes, and shoes, and even their physical frame forgot their natural infirmity: for the former did not wear out in the course of so long a time, nor did their feet swell although they made such long marches. Of physicians, and medicine, and all other concerns about that kind of art, there was no mention at all amongst them; so completely banished was infirmity of every kind: for it is said, "He brought them out with silver and gold; and there was not one feeble person among their tribes."[18] But like men who had quitted this world, and were transplanted to another and a better one, even so did they eat and drink, neither did the sun's ray when it waxed hot smite their heads; for the cloud parted them from the fiery beam, hovering all round them, and serving like a portable shelter for the whole body of the people. Neither at night did they need a torch to disperse the darkness, but they had the pillar of fire, a source of unspeakable light, supplying two needs, one by its shining, the other by directing the course of their journey; for it was not only luminous, but also conducted that countless host along the wilderness with more certainty than any human guide. And they journeyed not only upon land but also upon sea as if it had been dry land; and they made an audacious experiment upon the laws of nature by treading upon that angry sea, marching through it as if it had been the hard and resisting surface of a rock; and indeed when they placed their feet upon it the element became like solid earth, and gently sloping plains and fields;

---

18   Psalms 105:37.

but when it received their enemies it worked after the nature of sea; and to the Israelites indeed it served as a chariot, but to their enemies it became a grave; conveying the former across with ease, but drowning the latter with great violence. And the disorderly flood of water displayed the good order and subordination which marks reasonable and highly intelligent men, fulfilling the part at one time of a guardian, at another of an executioner, and exhibiting these opposites together on one day. What shall one say of the rocks which gave forth streams of water? What of the clouds of birds which covered the whole face of the earth by the number of their carcasses? What of the wonders in Egypt? What of the marvels in the wilderness? What of the triumphs and bloodless victories? For they subdued those who opposed them like men keeping a holiday rather than making war. And they vanquished their own masters without the use of arms; and overcame those who fought with them after they left Egypt by means of singing and music; and what they did was a festival rather than a campaign, a religious ceremony rather than a battle. For all these wonders took place not merely for the purpose of supplying their need, but also that the people might preserve more accurately the doctrine which Moses inculcated of the knowledge of God; and voices proclaiming the presence of their Master were uttered on all sides of them. For the sea loudly declared this, by becoming a road for them to march upon, and then turning into sea again; and the waters of the Nile uttered this voice when they were converted into the nature of blood; and the frogs, and the great army of locusts, and the caterpillar and blight declared the same thing to all the people; and the wonders in the desert, the manna, the pillar of fire, the cloud, the quails, and all the other incidents served them as a book, and writing which could never be effaced, echoing daily in their memory and resounding in their mind. Nevertheless after such great and remarkable providence, after all those unspeakable benefits, after such mighty miracles, after care indescribable, after continual teaching, after instruction by means of speech, and admonition by means of deeds, after glorious victories, after extraordinary triumphs, after abundant supply of food, after the plentiful production of water, after the ineffable glory with which they were invested in the eyes of the human race, being ungrateful and senseless they worshipped a calf, and paid reverence to the head of a bull, even when the memorials of God's benefits in Egypt were fresh in their minds, and they were still in actual enjoyment of many more.

14. But the Ninevites, although a barbarous and foreign people who had never participated in any of these benefits, small or great, neither words, nor wonders, nor works, when they saw a man who had been saved from shipwreck, who had never associated with them before, but appeared then for the first time, enter their city and say, "Yet three days and Nineveh shall be overthrown,"[19] were so converted and reformed by the mere sound of these words, and putting away

---

19   Jonah 3:4.

their former wickedness, advanced in the direction of virtue by the path of repentance, that they caused the sentence of God to be revoked, and arrested the threatened disturbance of their city, and averted the heaven-sent wrath, and were delivered from every kind of evil. "For," we read, "God saw that every man turned from his evil way, and was converted to the Lord."[20] How turned? I ask. Although their wickedness was great, their iniquity unspeakable, their moral sores difficult to heal, which was plainly shown by the prophet when he said, "Their wickedness ascended even unto the heaven,"[21] indicating by the distance of the place the magnitude of their wickedness; nevertheless such great iniquity which was piled up to such a height as to reach even to the heaven, all this in the course of three days in a brief moment of time through the effect of a few words, which they heard from the mouth of one man and he an unknown shipwrecked stranger, they so thoroughly abolished, removed out of sight, and put away, as to have the happiness of hearing the declaration, "God saw that every one turned from his evil way, and He repented of the evil which God said He would do them." Do you see that he who is temperate and watchful not only suffers no injury at the hands of man, but even turns back Heaven-sent wrath? whereas he who betrays himself and harms himself by his own doing, even if he receives countless benefits, reaps no great advantage. So, at least, the Jews were not profited

---

20   Jonah 3:10.
21   Jonah 1:2.

by those great miracles, nor on the other hand were the Ninevites harmed by having no share in them; but since they were inwardly well-disposed, having laid hold of a slight opportunity they became better, barbarians and foreigners though they were, ignorant of all divine revelation, and dwelling at a distance from Palestine.

15. Again, I ask, was the virtue of the "three children" corrupted by the troubles which beset them? Whilst they were still young, mere youths, of immature age, did they not undergo that grievous affliction of captivity? Did they not have to make a long journey from home, and when they had arrived in the foreign country, were they not cut off from fatherland and home and temple, and altar and sacrifices, and offerings, and drink offerings, and even the singing of psalms? For not only were they debarred from their home, but as a consequence from many forms of worship also. Were they not given up into the hands of barbarians, wolves rather than men? And, most painful calamity of all, when they had been banished into so distant and barbarous a country, and were suffering such a grievous captivity, were they not without teacher, without prophets, without ruler? "For," it is written, "there is no ruler, nor prophet, nor governor, nor place for offering before You and finding mercy."[22] Yes moreover they were cast into the royal palace, as upon some cliff and crag, and a sea full of rocks and reefs, being compelled to sail over that angry sea without a pilot or

---

22   Cf. Daniel 3:38 LXX, OSB.

signal man, or crew, or sails; and they were cooped up in the royal court as in a prison. For inasmuch as they knew spiritual wisdom, and were superior to worldly things, and despised all human pride and made the wings of their soul soar upwards, they counted their sojourn there as an aggravation of their trouble. For had they been outside the court, and dwelling in a private house, they would have enjoyed more independence; but having been cast into that prison (for they deemed the splendor of the palace no better than a prison, no safer than a place of rocks and crags), they were straightway subjected to cruel embarrassment. For the king commanded them to be partakers of his own table, a luxurious, unclean, and profane table, a thing which was forbidden them, and seemed more terrible than death; and they were lonely men hemmed in like lambs amongst so many wolves. And they were constrained to choose between being consumed by famine or rather led off to execution, and tasting of forbidden meats. What then did these youths do, forlorn as they were, captives, strangers, slaves of those who commanded these things? They did not consider that this strait or the absolute power of him who possessed the state sufficed to justify their compliance; but they employed every device and expedient to enable them to avoid the sin, although they were abandoned on every side. For they could not influence men by money: how should they, being captives? Nor by friendship and social intercourse? How should they, being strangers? Nor could they get the better of them by any exertion of power: how was it possible, being slaves? Nor master them by force of numbers: how could they, being only three? Therefore they approached the eunuch who possessed the necessary authority, and persuaded him by their arguments. For when they saw him fearful and trembling, and in an agony of alarm concerning his own safety, and the dread of death which agitated his soul was intolerable: "For I fear," said he, "my lord the king, lest he should see your countenances sadder than the children which are of your sort and so shall you endanger my head to the king,"[23] having released him from this fear they persuaded him to grant them the favor. And since they brought to the work all the strength which they had, God also henceforth contributed His strength to it. For it was not God's doing only that they achieved those things for the sake of which they were to receive a reward, but the beginning and starting point was from their own purpose, and having manifested that to be noble and brave, they won for themselves the help of God, and so accomplished their aim.

16. Do you then perceive that if a man does not injure himself, no one else will be able to harm him? Behold at least youthfulness, and captivity and destitution, and removal into a foreign land, and loneliness, and lack of protectors, and a stern command, and great fear of death assailing the mind of the eunuch, and poverty, and feebleness of numbers, and dwelling in the midst of barbarians, and having enemies for masters, and surrender into the hands of the king himself, and

---

23   Daniel 1:10.

separation from all their kindred, and removal from priests and prophets, and from all others who cared for them, and the cessation of drink offerings and sacrifices, and loss of the temple and psalmody, and yet none of these things harmed them; but they had more renown then than when they enjoyed these things in their native land. And after they had accomplished this task first and had wreathed their brows with the glorious garland of victory, and had kept the law even in a foreign land, and trampled under foot the tyrant's command, and overcome fear of the avenger, and yet received no harm from any quarter, as if they had been quietly living at home and enjoying the benefit of all those things which I mentioned, after they had thus fearlessly accomplished their work they were again summoned to other contests. And again they were the same men; and they were subjected to a more severe trial than the former one, and a furnace was kindled, and they were confronted by the barbarian army in company with the king; and the whole Persian force was set in motion and everything was devised which tended to put deceit or constraint upon them: varying kinds of music, and various forms of punishment, and threats, and what they saw on every side of them was alarming, and the words which they heard were more alarming than what they saw; nevertheless since they did not betray themselves, but made the most of their own strength, they never sustained any kind of damage, but even won for themselves more glorious crowns of victory than before. For Nebuchadnezzar bound them and cast them into the furnace, yet he burnt them not, but rather benefited them, and rendered them more illustrious. And although they were deprived of temple (for I will repeat my former remarks) and altar, and fatherland, and priests and prophets, although they were in a foreign and barbarous country, in the very midst of the furnace, surrounded by all that mighty host, the king himself who did this looking on, they set up a glorious trophy, and won a notable victory, having sung that admirable and extraordinary hymn which from that day to this has been sung throughout the world and will continue to be sung to future generations.

Thus then when a man does not injure himself, he cannot possibly be hurt by another, for I will not cease harping constantly upon this saying. For if captivity, and bondage, and loneliness and loss of country and all kindred, and death, and burning, and a great army and a savage tyrant could not do any damage to the innate virtue of the three children captives, bondmen, strangers though they were in a foreign land, but the enemy's assault became to them rather the occasion of greater confidence: what shall be able to harm the temperate man? There is nothing, even should he have the whole world in arms against him. But, someone may say, in their case God stood beside them, and plucked them out of the flame. Certainly He did; and if you will play your part to the best of your power, the help which God supplies will assuredly follow.

17. Nevertheless the reason why I admire those youths, and pronounce them blessed, and enviable, is not because they tramped on the flame, and vanquished the force of the fire, but because they were bound, and cast into the furnace, and delivered to the fire for the sake of true doctrine. For this it was which constituted the completeness of their triumph, and the wreath of victory was placed on their brows as soon as they were cast into the furnace and before the issue of events it began to be weaved for them from the moment that they uttered those words which they spoke with much boldness and freedom of speech to the king when they were brought into his presence. "We have no need to answer you concerning this thing; for our God in Heaven, whom we serve, is able to rescue us out of the burning fiery furnace; and He will deliver us out of your hands, O King. But if not, be it known unto you, O King, that we will not serve your gods nor worship the golden image which you have set up."[24] After the utterance of these words, I proclaimed them conquerors; after these words having grasped the prize of victory, they hastened on to the glorious crown of martyrdom, following up the confession which they made through their words with the confession made through their deeds. But if when they had been cast into it, the fire had respect for their bodies, and undid their bonds, and suffered them to go down into it without fear, and forgot its natural force, so that the furnace of fire became as a fountain of cool water, this

24 Daniel 3:16–18.

marvel was the effect of God's grace and of the divine wonder-working power. Yet the heroes themselves, even before these things took place, as soon as they set foot in the flames, had erected their trophy, and won their victory and put on their crown, and had been proclaimed conquerors both in Heaven and on earth, and so far as they were concerned, nothing was wanting for their renown.

What then would you have to say to these things? Have you been driven into exile, and expelled from your country? Behold so also were they. Have you suffered captivity, and become the servant of barbarian masters? Well! this also you will find befell these men. But you have no one present there to regulate your state nor to advise or instruct you? Well! of attention of this kind these men were destitute. Or you have been bound, burned, put to death? for you cannot tell me of anything more painful than these things. Yet behold! these men having gone through them all, were made more glorious by each one of them, yes, more exceedingly illustrious, and increased the store of their treasures in Heaven. And the Jews indeed who had both temple, and altar, and ark and cherubim, and mercy-seat, and veil, and an infinite multitude of priests, and daily services, and morning and evening sacrifices, and continually heard the voices of the prophets, both living and departed, sounding in their ears, and carried about with them the recollection of the wonders which were done in Egypt, and in the wilderness, and all the rest, and turned the story of these things over in their hands, and had them inscribed upon their door posts and enjoyed the benefit at that time of much supernatural power and every other kind of help were yet no wise profited, but rather damaged, having set up idols in the temple itself, and having sacrificed their sons and daughters under trees, and in almost every part of the country in Palestine having offered those unlawful and accursed sacrifices, and perpetrated countless other deeds yet more monstrous. But these men, although in the midst of a barbarous and hostile land, having their occupation in a tyrant's house, deprived of all that care of which I have been speaking, led away to execution, and subjected to burning, not only suffered no harm there from small or great, but became the more illustrious. Knowing then these things, and collecting instances of the like kind from the inspired divine Scriptures (for it is possible to find many such examples in the case of various other persons), we deem that neither a difficulty arising from seasons or events, nor compulsion and force, nor the arbitrary authority of rulers[25], furnish a sufficient excuse for us when we transgress. I will now conclude my discourse by repeating what I said at the beginning, that if any one be harmed and injured he certainly suffers this at his own hands, not at the hands of others even if there be countless multitudes injuring and insulting him, so that if he does not suffer this at his own hands, not all the creatures who inhabit the whole earth and sea if they combined to attack him would be able to hurt one who is vigilant and sober in the Lord.

---

25   Original translation: potentates.

Let us then, I beseech you, be sober and vigilant at all times, and let us endure all painful things bravely that we may obtain those everlasting and pure blessings in Christ Jesus our Lord, to whom be glory and power, now and ever throughout all ages. Amen.